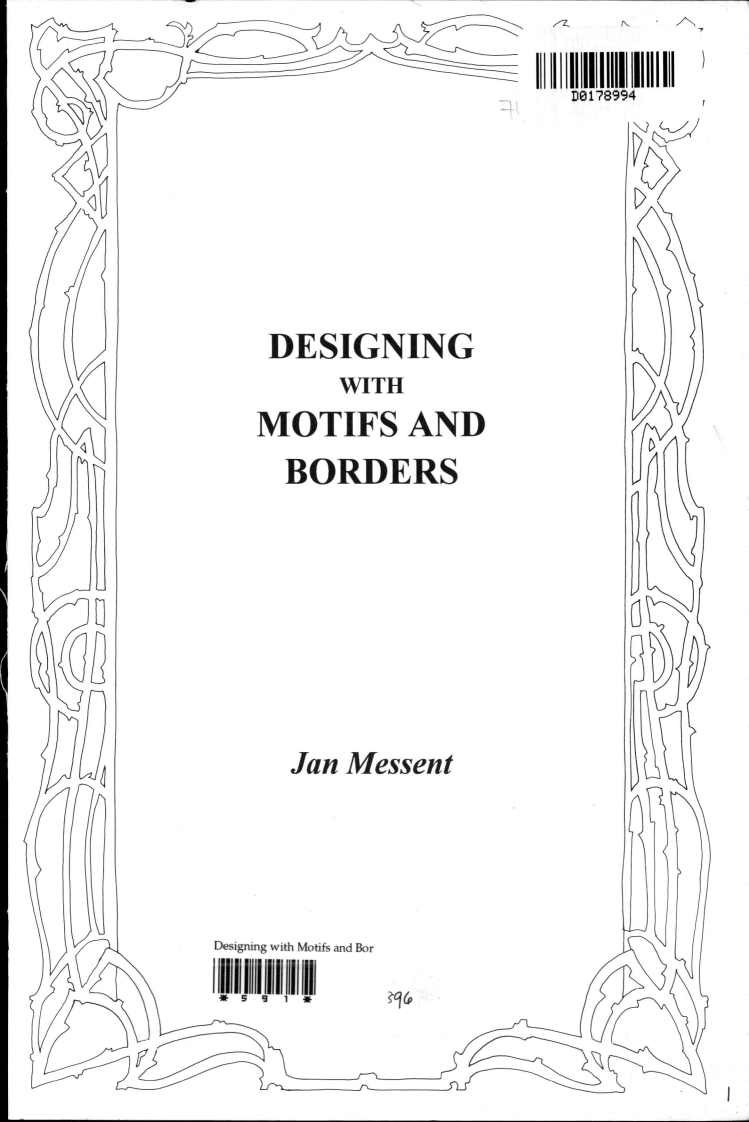

DESIGNING
WITH
MOTIFS AND
BORDERS

Jan Messent

Observe: a garden
seat with a simple
pattern of over-lapping
curves.

Explore: sketch this
arrangement on
squared paper in
different positions.

Invent: various ways of shading will bring out some of
the formations inside the lines. Many interpretations
are possible.

Book cover: Juliet Williams   1896

2

Integrated Borders

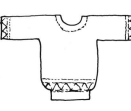

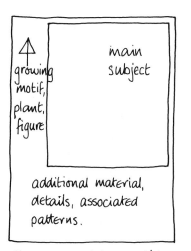

Borders should not be regarded as after-thoughts, they should be seen as a part of the design as early as the initial concept stage.

We are used to seeing borders around the extremities of things. But ask yourself how they can play a more important role within the main subject, for example, or by taking a different direction from the more usual one.

This helps to focus the attention and, in the case of the picture, places the main subject in a more "precious" space. The borders on the garment are more unusual than the bands around hips and wrists.

Old manuscripts use this arrangement a good deal. It may even be interesting to see the border run into the main subject.

Borders everywhere : wide panels of different widths allow space for extra information, patterns, etc..

Borders used as dividers to separate different elements of the same subject, e.g. five senses, four elements, three graces.

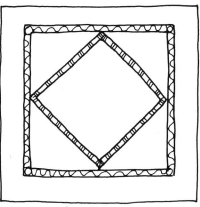

A format like this could contain a tree, plant, figure or any other tall motif surrounded by more of its own kind, or details.

Main subject in centre square (perhaps in miniature?) enclosed by patterns, symbols of affection, good fortune, religion, numbers, words.

Borders within borders.
a. Main theme in centre, subordinate material in triangles.
b. Spread main theme into all five sections.
c. Spread main theme to outer edges and use the borders both as a diversion and a focussing device.

Migrating reindeer from the border of the Pazyryk Carpet. Scythian. c. 500 B.C.
   A border of star-shapes, possibly stylized snowflakes, separates the outer and inner borders.
Horses and riders, alternately riding and walking, are from the same carpet.

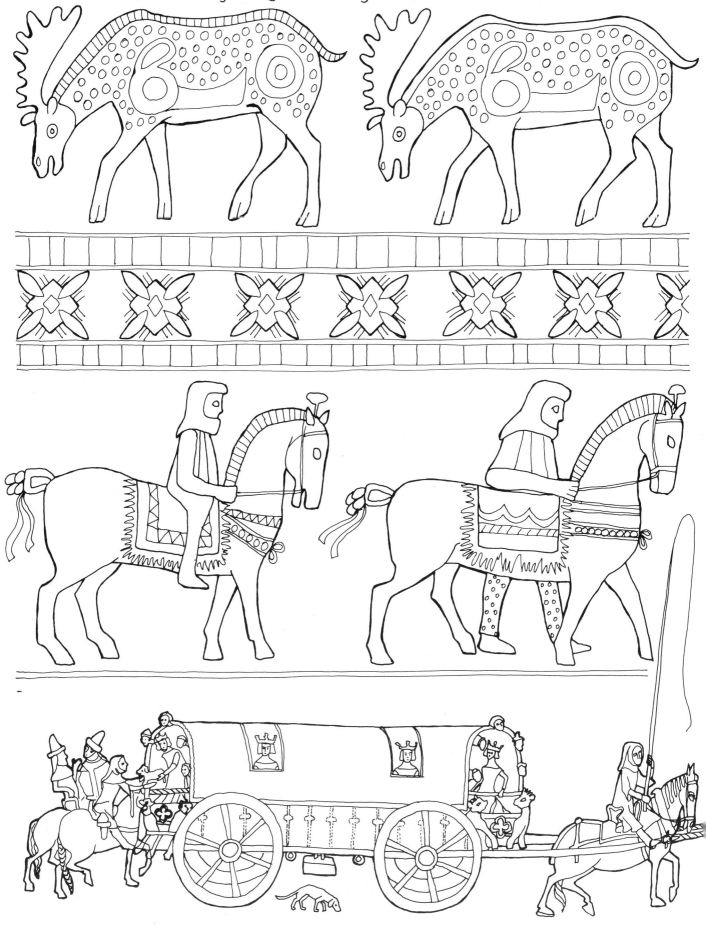

A travelling carriage for royal ladies, from the Luttrell Psalter. Early 14th century.

Border Definitions

A band or margin around or along the edge of something.
A design or ornamental strip around the rim of something, e.g. page or plate.
A long narrow strip of ground planted with flowers, skirting a path.
Boundary, trimming, precinct, out-skirts, periphery, marchland/marches, valance, selvedge, binding, fringe, hem, rim, trim, verge, frontier, margin, confine, limit.

Border States: Delaware, Kentucky, Maryland, Missouri, Virginia.

Border Collie, Border Terrier (both dog breeds), Border Leicester (sheep breed), border guard, lodger (boarder), borderline case, borderline failure, bordering on the ridiculous, bordering on madness, the boundaries of good taste, the fringes of society, out of bounds, off-limit, brass-band, making tracks, following-on, following in father's footsteps, grandmother's footsteps.

Progressing Borders : Footprints, barefoot or shoe-prints
Animal tracks, hoof prints, etc.
Bird tracks, snail-trails, snake-tracks, lines of insects, flights of birds and bees.
People and animals following / chasing each other or linked together, dancing, playing games, processions, rituals, etc..
Animal caravans, gypsies, horses, camels, elephants, zoo rides.

Mechanical: Cars, trains, other vehicles following. Tyre tracks.
Static/linking: Pathways, roads, bridle-paths, maps, rivers, streams, Stepping stones, walls, railings, fences.
Chains, ropes. Daisy chain, garland, circular posies.
Words / lettering — continuous sentence or repeated word.
Linked hands.

British Museum. There are numerous other examples to be seen in this manuscript.

5

6

If you are not comfortable with plain white paper and a pencil, consider using other means of repeating shapes, such as folded and cut paper, (paper-bags, newsprint, wall-paper, magazine-cuttings, etc.,), potato-prints, torn paper strips/cut-up photocopies, stencils and templates, fibre-pens, coloured pencils, paints, wax-crayons, pastels, or any combination of these. Some of these media are used on the opposite page. Coloured paper is a kinder background to these methods than white paper. A good variety can be found in scrap-books and pads used for pastel crayons.

Both stencil and template can be used for drawing an outline of a shape, but with paint or crayon, the stencil will produce a positive image and the template will leave a negative one.

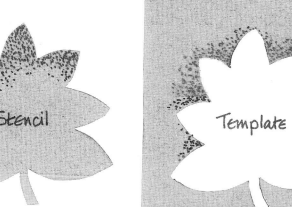

Stencil

Template

Research.

Ideas for design often arise from an interest which may have been forming in the mind for years. During this time, information may have been collected in a folder or scrapbook, waiting to be collated and examined for useful starting-points, interpretations and developments.

Materials may include drawings/ sketches, photographs, cuttings, adverts and associated words. Even words which share only the same <u>sound</u> are useful as springboards to launch an idea into another dimension. Find out all you can about your chosen subject. Make notes. Everything you discover will give you more ideas about how your material can be used.

Fan: an ardent admirer. Fan-mail. Fantastic. Fan-light, fan-tailed, fan belt, fanatic, fantasy, fanfare, fandango, fantasia, fanciful, fan-dance, fan-heater, fancy.

The fan-shaped lace collar of Queen Elizabeth I from a portrait by John Bettes II (attrib.) c. 1585—90.

The pleated head-dress of a Venetian carnival costume. (Photo: Sylvia Cosh)

Fan-vaulting

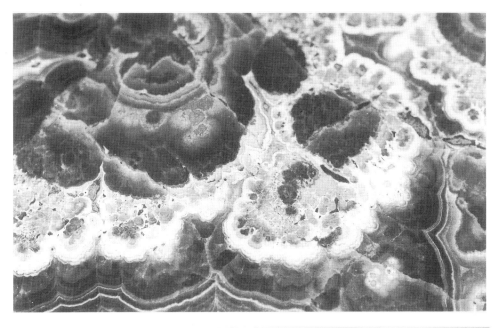

Fan-shaped clusters of lichen (photo Sandra Goode).

Detail from an advertisement.

Broken fan-shapes in agate.

The underside of a water-lily leaf.

One of the royal heraldic beasts at Hampton Court Palace. Surrey.

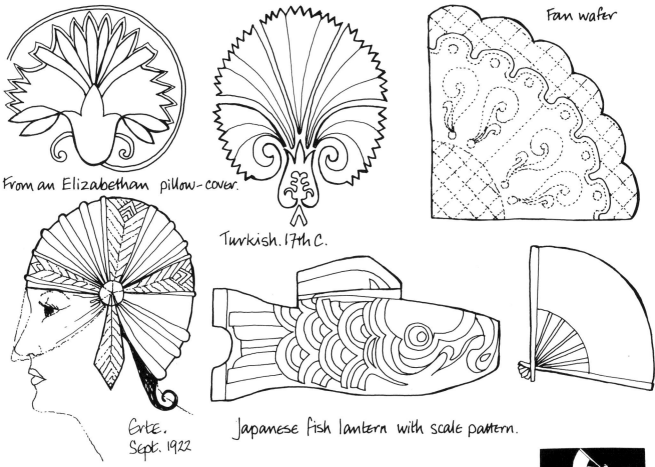

From an Elizabethan pillow-cover.

Turkish. 17th C.

Fan wafer

Erté.
Sept. 1922

Japanese fish lantern with scale pattern.

Below: detail from an embroidered panel dated 1751. V. & A. Museum.

Having gathered our source material together, what are we to do with it?
We study it, analyse it, and use it as a 'bank' for ideas. All the sketches on this page were made directly from the material on the previous pages, and although I know what shape a fan is, and something of its structure, I could never have devised all these ways of decorating it without this extra information. We borrow ideas from every available source and adapt them to our own purposes.

Drawing is not used here to practice a skill but to a) help you look more closely (you have to do this to draw it), and b) to make a visual record of what you see.

You can then go forward and "doodle" with fan shapes knowing that you have a store of ideas to clothe the bare-bones of a design.

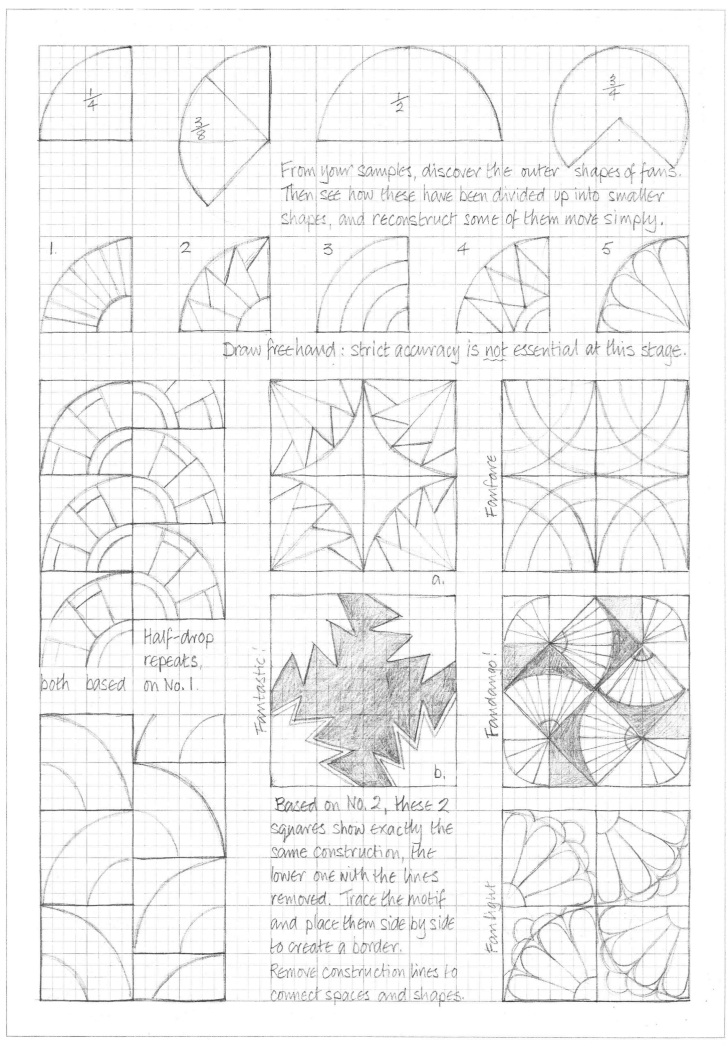

¼

⅜

½

¾

From your samples, discover the outer shapes of fans. Then see how these have been divided up into smaller shapes, and reconstruct some of them more simply.

1.　2.　3.　4.　5.

Draw free-hand: strict accuracy is *not* essential at this stage.

both based

Half-drop repeats, on No. 1.

on No. 1.

Fanfare

a.

Fantastic!

b.

Fandango!

Fanlight

Based on No. 2, these 2 squares show exactly the same construction, the lower one with the lines removed. Trace the motif and place them side by side to create a border.

Remove construction lines to connect spaces and shapes.

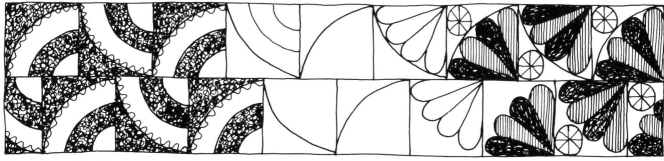

Based on No.3

Based on No.5 — small circle added

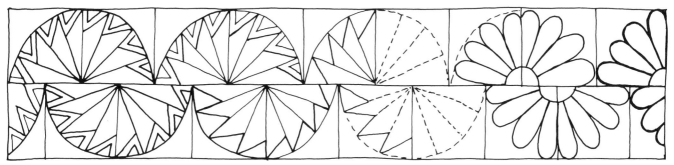

Based on No.2 — looks particularly good when seen vertically

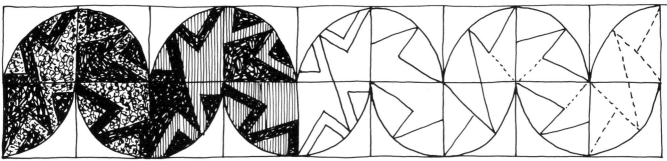

Based on No.2 with fewer 'spines'.   Look at each quarter-circle individually

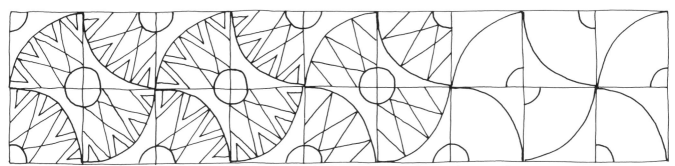

Based on No.4. A more complex version of the ancient "double-axe" pattern

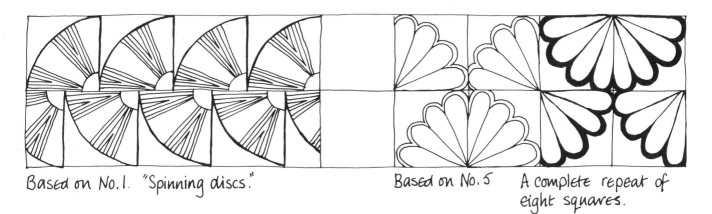

Based on No.1. "Spinning discs."

Based on No.5   A complete repeat of eight squares.

In the past, when functional
objects tended to be of a geo-
metrical nature, chests, boxes,
combs, sheilds, garments, bags,
rugs, coffins, buildings, books,
etc., the decoration used upon
them was usually designed to
fit, either as one motif or a coll-
ection, quite often bordered.
Even motifs derived from very
un-geometrical sources, flowers,
animals, etc., were shaped and
contorted to fit the space
available.

A stone grave-slab, only partly
completed, from 9th century
York.

Above left:
'A phesant'. One of the panels at
Oxburgh Hall, Norfolk, embroidered by Mary, Queen of Scots. The
motif, taken from a woodcut by
Gesner, would not fit into the
cruciform shape, so the startled
bird's tail was chopped off and
placed above him.

In the lower panel, also by Mary,
the turnip fits more happily into
its octogon.

It is worth bearing in mind
that either the motif will determine the shape which encloses it,
or the shape will determine the
motif.   Nowadays, of course,
not all motifs are enclosed.

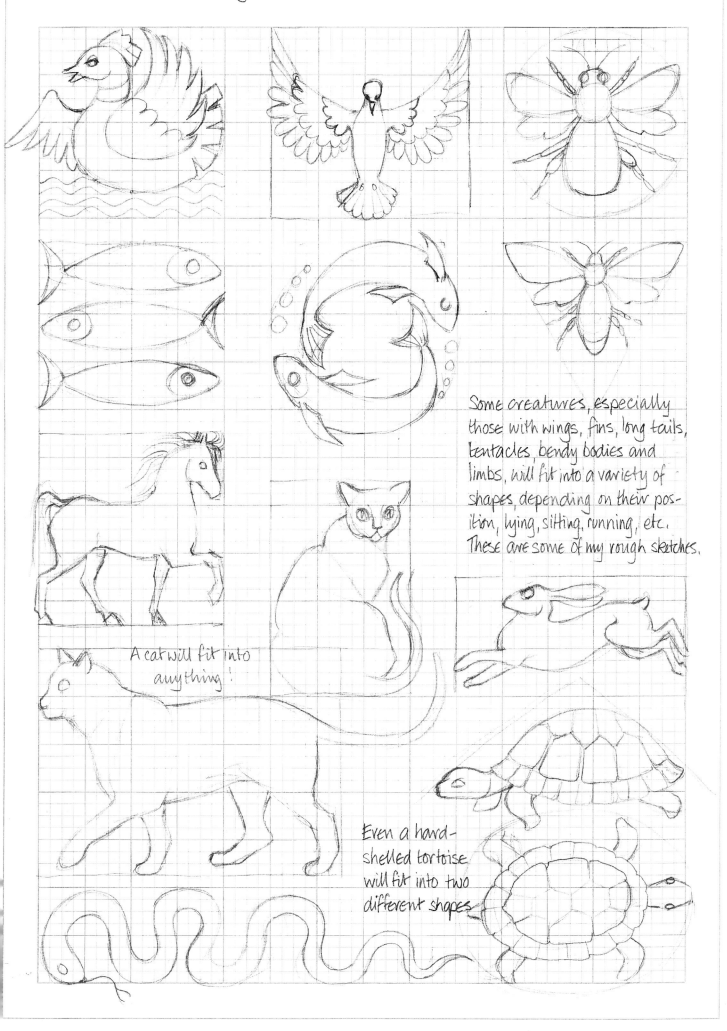

Some creatures, especially those with wings, fins, long tails, tentacles, bendy bodies and limbs, will fit into a variety of shapes, depending on their position, lying, sitting, running, etc. These are some of my rough sketches.

A cat will fit into anything!

Even a hard-shelled tortoise will fit into two different shapes

The designs on the opposite page have been derived from simple letter-forms. More intricate styles will produce even more interesting and complex arrangements, whether for borders or for single units. The letter-motifs shown here are from historic sources, some of them now almost abstract.

14th century Italian

10th – 11th century English

12th century English.

16th century   Italian

German

10th century English

8th century Irish (Book of Kells)

8th century Irish (Kells)

16

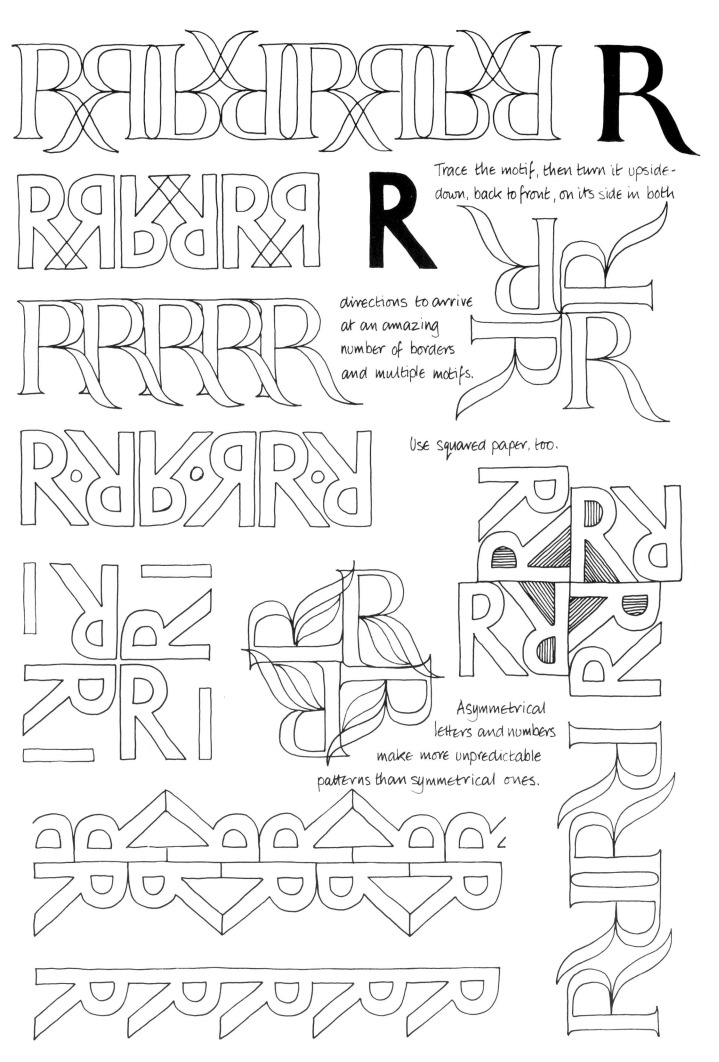

R

R

Trace the motif, then turn it upside-down, back to front, on its side in both directions to arrive at an amazing number of borders and multiple motifs.

Use squared paper, too.

Asymmetrical letters and numbers make more unpredictable patterns than symmetrical ones.

Resolving the Corners

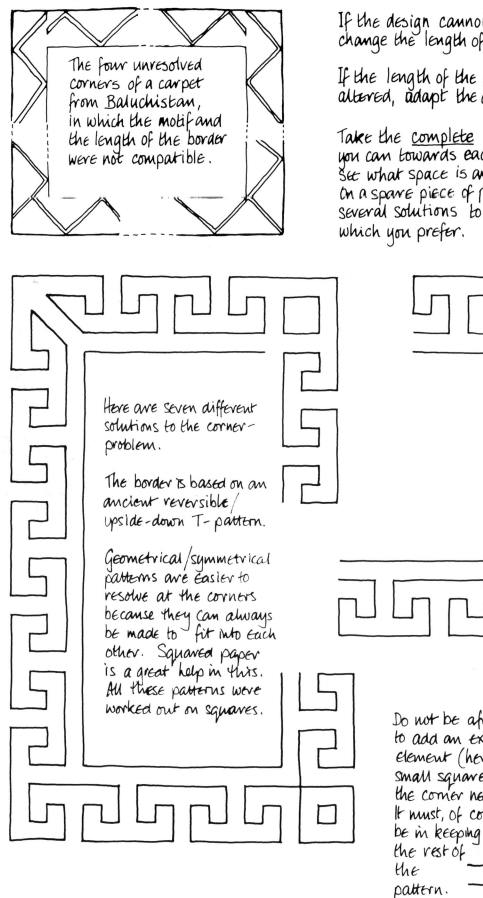

The four unresolved corners of a carpet from Baluchistan, in which the motif and the length of the border were not compatible.

If the design cannot be adapted, change the length of the border to fit.

If the length of the border cannot be altered, adapt the design to fit it.

Take the __complete__ motifs as far as you can towards each corner and then see what space is available.
On a spare piece of paper, try out several solutions to the problem to see which you prefer.

Here are seven different solutions to the corner-problem.

The border is based on an ancient reversible/upside-down T-pattern.

Geometrical/symmetrical patterns are easier to resolve at the corners because they can always be made to fit into each other. Squared paper is a great help in this. All these patterns were worked out on squares.

Do not be afraid to add an extra element (here, a small square) if the corner needs it. It must, of course, be in keeping with the rest of the pattern.

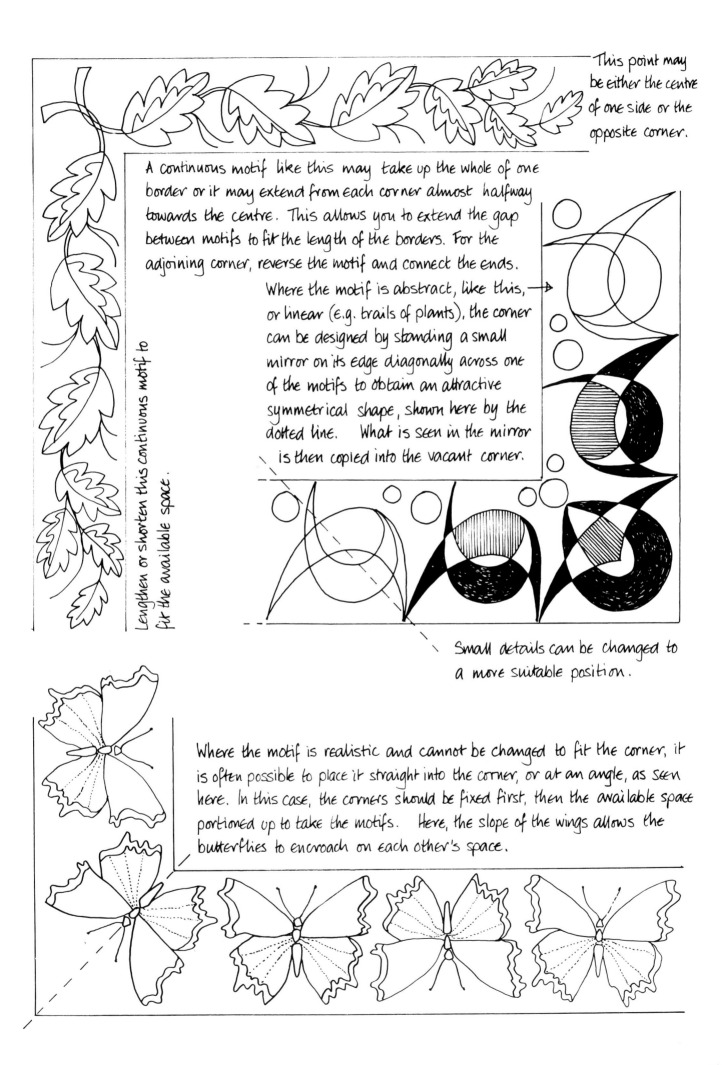

This point may be either the centre of one side or the opposite corner.

A continuous motif like this may take up the whole of one border or it may extend from each corner almost halfway towards the centre. This allows you to extend the gap between motifs to fit the length of the borders. For the adjoining corner, reverse the motif and connect the ends.

Where the motif is abstract, like this, → or linear (e.g. trails of plants), the corner can be designed by standing a small mirror on its edge diagonally across one of the motifs to obtain an attractive symmetrical shape, shown here by the dotted line. What is seen in the mirror is then copied into the vacant corner.

Lengthen or shorten this continuous motif to fit the available space.

Small details can be changed to a more suitable position.

Where the motif is realistic and cannot be changed to fit the corner, it is often possible to place it straight into the corner, or at an angle, as seen here. In this case, the corners should be fixed first, then the available space portioned up to take the motifs. Here, the slope of the wings allows the butterflies to encroach on each other's space.

The One-way-up Border

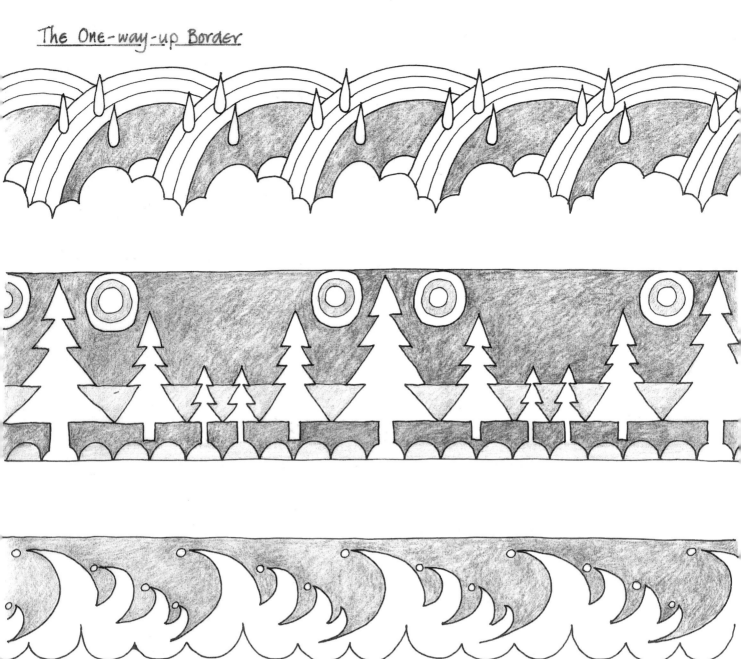

Some motifs have a 'one-way-up' restriction, trees, scenery, waves/water, people and animals. Other subjects, birds, insects, planets and flower-heads, for example, can be seen from any angle. The design of the side borders must therefore be thought about at the beginning, perhaps by changing to some other relevant motif.

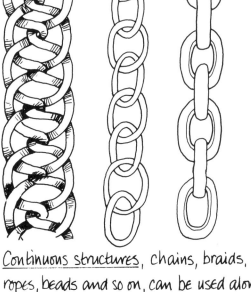

Continuous structures, chains, braids,
ropes, beads and so on, can be used alone or in conjunction
with other elements. This idea has been used since earliest
times and in many cultures. Look at buildings: the
Victorians, especially, delighted in such details.

How to Reduce a Design to the Same Proportions

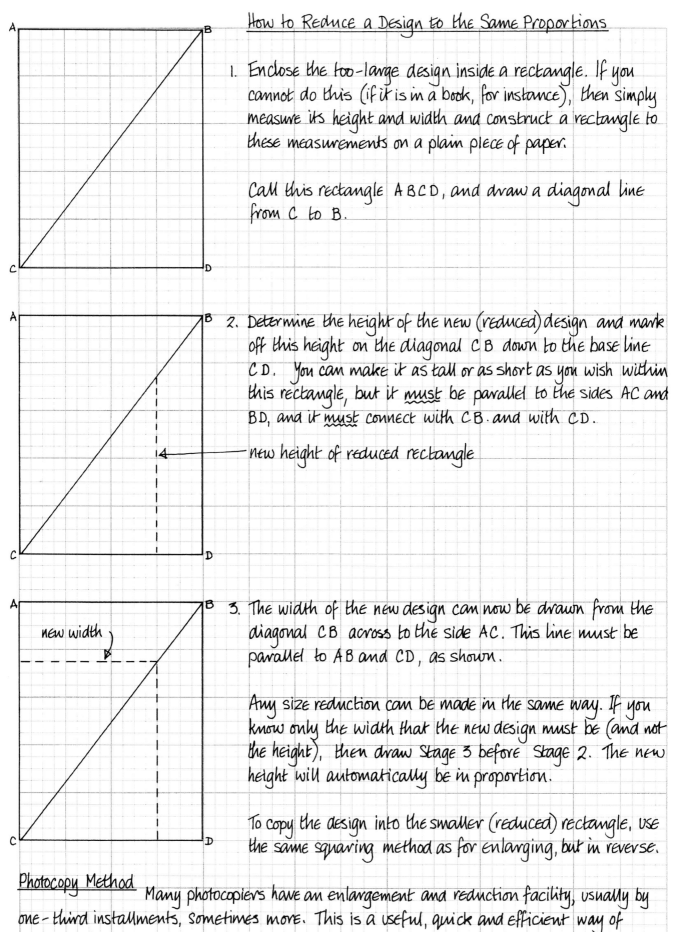

1. Enclose the too-large design inside a rectangle. If you cannot do this (if it is in a book, for instance), then simply measure its height and width and construct a rectangle to these measurements on a plain piece of paper.

   Call this rectangle A B C D, and draw a diagonal line from C to B.

2. Determine the height of the new (reduced) design and mark off this height on the diagonal C B down to the base line C D. You can make it as tall or as short as you wish within this rectangle, but it must be parallel to the sides AC and BD, and it must connect with C B. and with C D.

   — new height of reduced rectangle

3. The width of the new design can now be drawn from the diagonal C B across to the side AC. This line must be parallel to AB and CD, as shown.

   Any size reduction can be made in the same way. If you know only the width that the new design must be (and not the height), then draw Stage 3 before Stage 2. The new height will automatically be in proportion.

   To copy the design into the smaller (reduced) rectangle, use the same squaring method as for enlarging, but in reverse.

new width

Photocopy Method

Many photocopiers have an enlargement and reduction facility, usually by one-third installments, sometimes more. This is a useful, quick and efficient way of changing the dimensions of even the most complex design. Ask at any photocopy shop for details and charges. Libraries have photocopiers, too.

How to Enlarge a Design to the Same Proportions

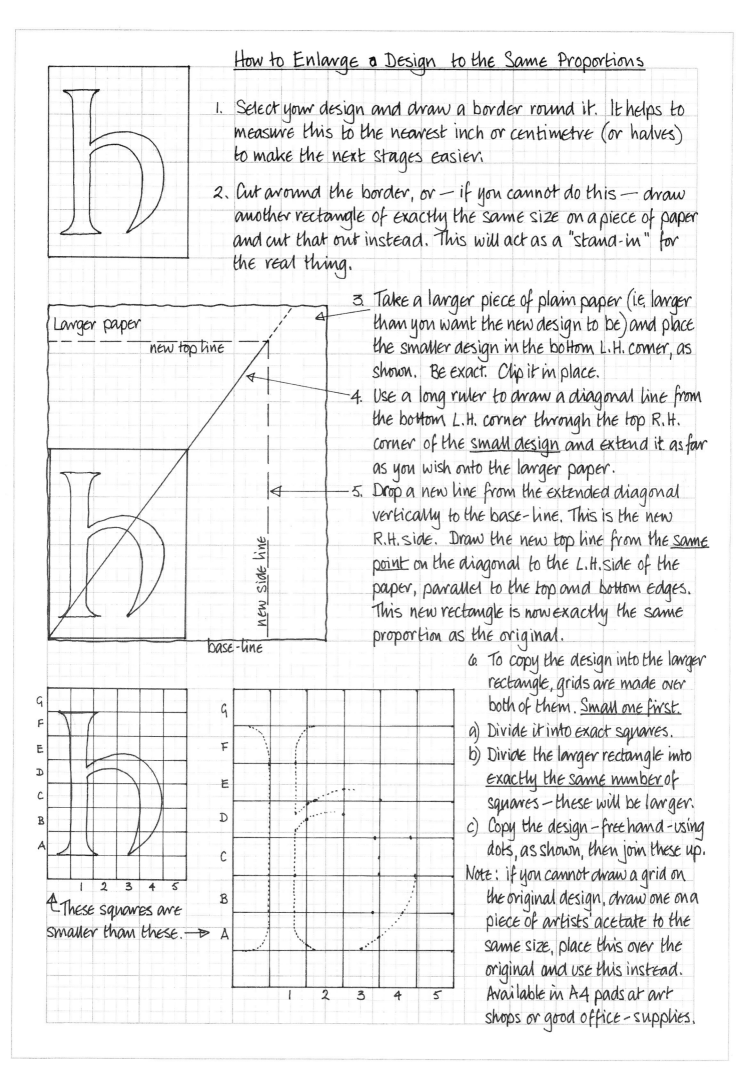

1. Select your design and draw a border round it. It helps to measure this to the nearest inch or centimetre (or halves) to make the next stages easier.

2. Cut around the border, or — if you cannot do this — draw another rectangle of exactly the same size on a piece of paper and cut that out instead. This will act as a "stand-in" for the real thing.

3. Take a larger piece of plain paper (i.e. larger than you want the new design to be) and place the smaller design in the bottom L.H. corner, as shown. Be exact. Clip it in place.

4. Use a long ruler to draw a diagonal line from the bottom L.H. corner through the top R.H. corner of the <u>small design</u> and extend it as far as you wish onto the larger paper.

5. Drop a new line from the extended diagonal vertically to the base-line. This is the new R.H. side. Draw the new top line from the <u>same point</u> on the diagonal to the L.H. side of the paper, parallel to the top and bottom edges. This new rectangle is now exactly the same proportion as the original.

6. To copy the design into the larger rectangle, grids are made over both of them. <u>Small one first.</u>

a) Divide it into exact squares.

b) Divide the larger rectangle into <u>exactly the same number of</u> squares — these will be larger.

c) Copy the design — free hand — using dots, as shown, then join these up.

Note: if you cannot draw a grid on the original design, draw one on a piece of artists' acetate to the same size, place this over the original and use this instead. Available in A4 pads at art shops or good office-supplies.

Larger paper

new top line

new side line

base-line

G F E D C B A
1 2 3 4 5

← These squares are smaller than these. →

G F E D C B A
1 2 3 4 5

23

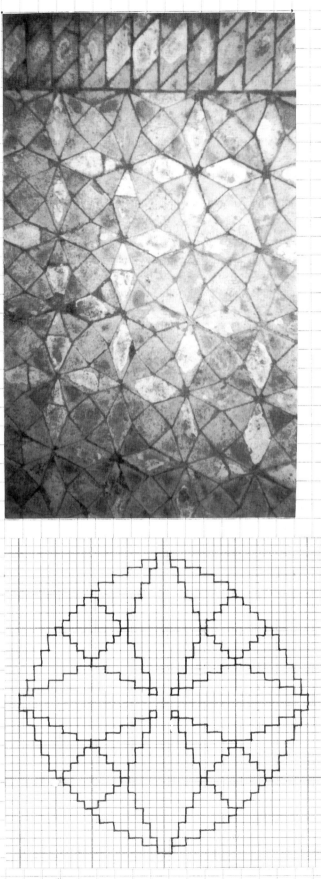

How to Make a Chart from a Motif

Left: a pattern of 13th century tiles from Fountains Abbey, North Yorkshire.

<u>Stage One</u>
The motif is produced by overlapping circles. Study the construction to isolate the motif.

The circles have been translated into straight-sided shapes. This makes it easier to chart.

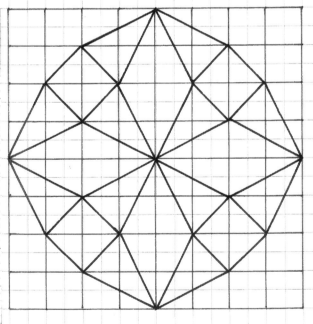

<u>Stage Two</u>
Use squared paper to re-draw the shape. The lines of this symmetrical motif are drawn across only one or two squares.

As near as possible, draw this stage to the size you want the finished chart to be, to avoid enlarging or reducing later.

<u>Stage Three</u>
Using tracing graph-paper (for preference), trace the motif onto the squares as near to the lines as possible. With a symmetrical design like this, each quarter must be exactly the same. All points have to be translated as squares ; four points that meet will make a larger square.

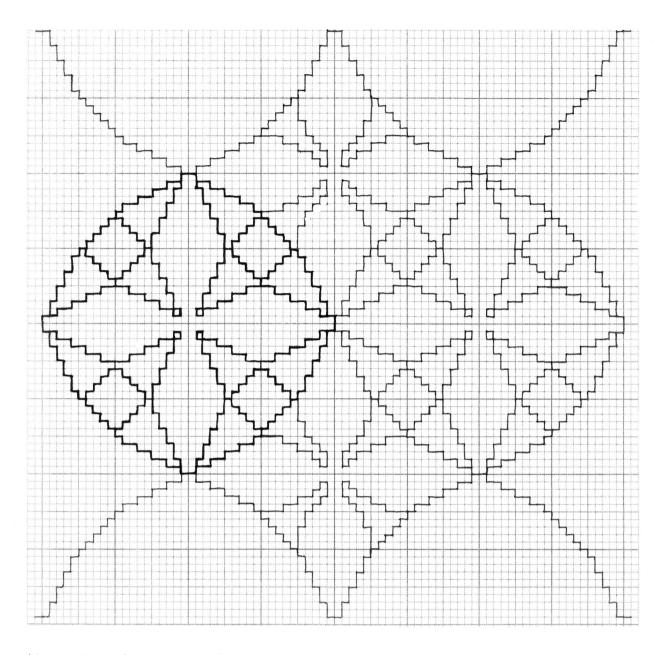

Notice how the problem of 'points-into-squares' has been dealt with in these examples. Because the now blunted points take more room up, the curved diamond-shape between each main motif is not exactly the same size as the ones inside, but slightly smaller, and though the leaf-shapes are the same width, the triangles between are not. Even so, the main motif fits its counterpart and the overall effect is maintained. A simple border-pattern can easily be constructed from the leaf shapes and squares. Make this as simple or as complex as you wish.

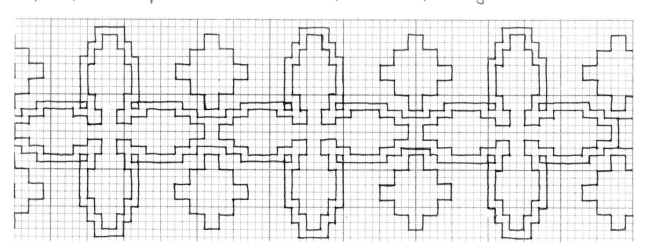

Medieval tile patterns are an excellent source of material for motifs, borders and all-over patterns. Often, they were designed to link on two or all four sides, circles being a favourite linking device. They are perfect for cushions and clothing.

Useful book on this subject :
English Medieval Tiles
Elizabeth Eames   ISBN
pub. British Museum. 0 7141 2029 4

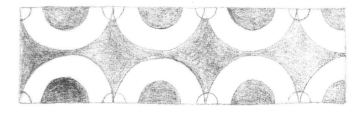

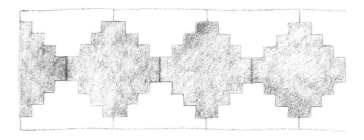

Stage One : the original sketch of four tiles.

Stage Two (above): enlarge one tile as shown on page 23.   Tidy the motif up at the same time, perfecting the quarter-circles with a compass or a cup or saucer.

If you prefer, this stage can be omitted. Go straight on to Stage 3 — i.e. make the enlargement straight onto graph-paper instead of plain paper.

Rub out unwanted lines or use typists' correcting fluid on pen lines. Keep a copy of the original enlargement. Use coloured pencils rather than paint.

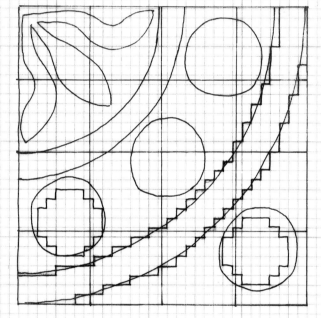

Stage Three (above): redraw the enlargement onto graph paper in the same way (i.e. by squaring the paper, as shown).

Now go over the drawn lines, "stepping" them over onto the graph lines where they coincide. Some small changes will have to be made where shapes refuse to fit into spaces.

Stage Four (right)
If you want the circles to join exactly where each of the four tiles meet, be sure to count the squares and place the ends at the same places on the outer edge.

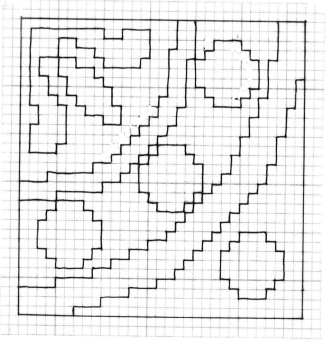

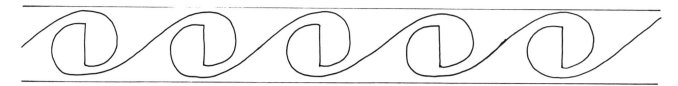

Geometric Patterns : Motifs and Borders

Right: The
Hunterston Brooch.
Celtic. 8th century.

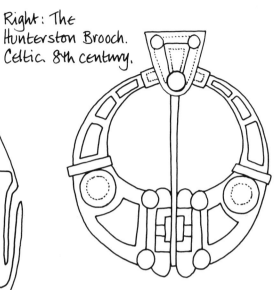

Left: A cast bronze coin inscribed
in the new Mogul alphabet for the
Kublai Khan (d. 1215)

Below: a 16th century applique
pattern from Finland.

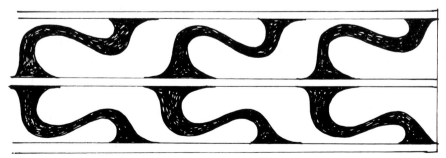

Stone design: 5th – 6th century. Swedish.

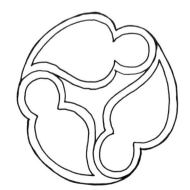

14th C. tile pattern.

1. Border from an Arita jar of c.1680 : Japan.

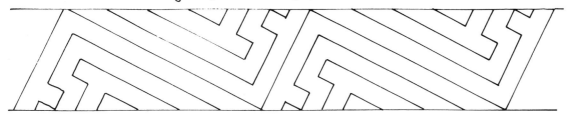

2.

2. Linking motifs taken from an Italian velvet of the 17th C.

3. Motif from the centre of a gold pendant. Hedeby. (Danish Viking)

4. 5th – 6th century Swedish stone border design.

5. Pottery design from Athens. c. 720 – 700 B.C.

6. Design from an Icelandic woven bedspread. 18th C.

3.

4.

6.

5.

<u>Elizabethan</u> and Italian
knot gardens consisted of
low clipped hedges in intricate patterns.

The borders and motifs on the
opposite page are all compo-
sed of single elements
derived from these more
complicated square patterns.

No matter how complex, a
motif can usually be sep-
arated into simple units
which can then be isolated
and repeated to make
borders.

Turn squares round to make
diamonds, and arrange
them side by side, just touch-
ing, or over-lapping the
corners.

Patterns of box hedges on the lawn at Cliveden, Bucks., consist of one repeating element with conical evergreens in the spaces.
On the right of this page, the pattern has been charted.

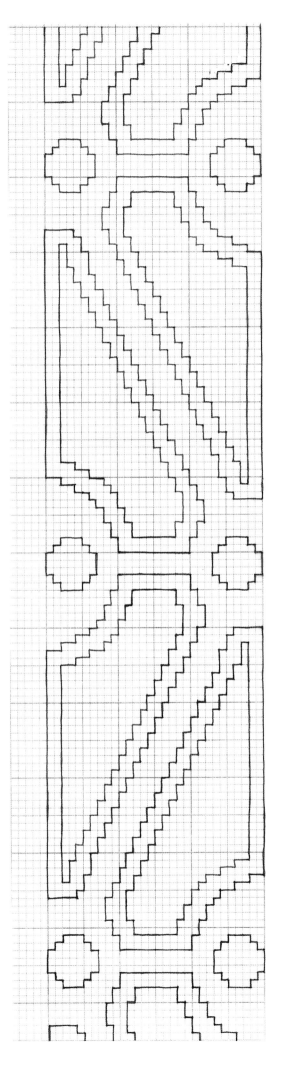

Floral Motifs

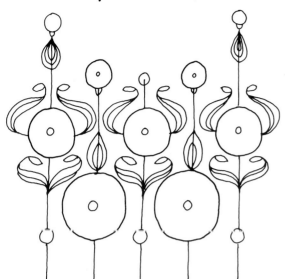

A simplified drawing of a book-cover design by Sarah MacConnell, published by The Studio in 1897.

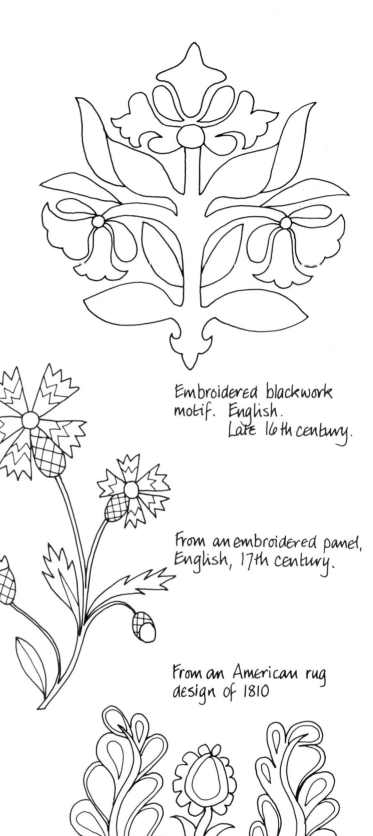

Embroidered blackwork motif. English. Late 16th century.

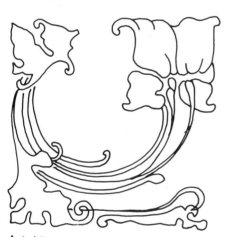

Art Nouveau.

From an embroidered panel, English, 17th century.

From an American rug design of 1810

Japanese.

Designs for embroiderers to use. c.1600. Victoria and Albert Museum.

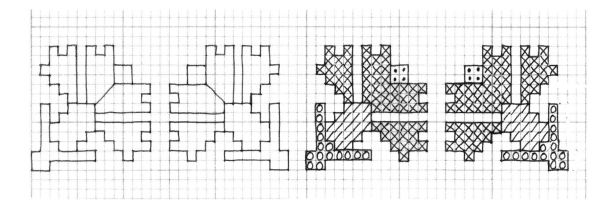

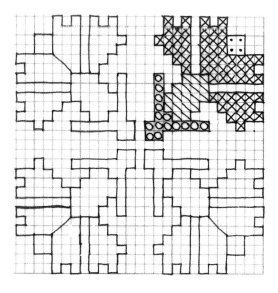

For charting in black and white —
use distinctive un-ambiguous symbols
such as x / o ▨ •   These represent
five colours ; any more than that will
probably require actual colours.
Coloured pencils are useful for this.

Flower-heads from an embroidered sampler.
Mid 17th century.

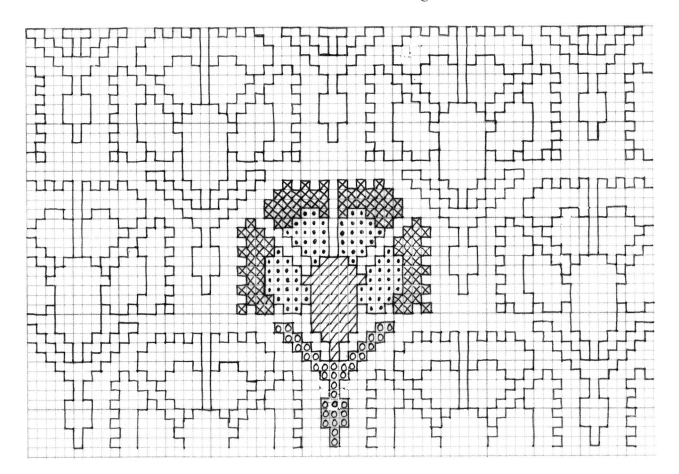

Stylised swirling leaves carved in sandstone on a capital in Alston Hall, Lancashire.

Plant-forms can be both static and moving. Look at the examples on this page and note how they fit into both categories.

Detail of cut tilework. Persia 15th century. below —

French Gothic

From a Coptic roundel. 7th – 8th century

Simple growth forms

Below: bowl decoration by Frederick Hurten Rhead. c. 1915

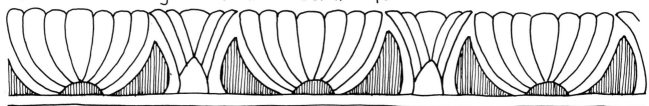

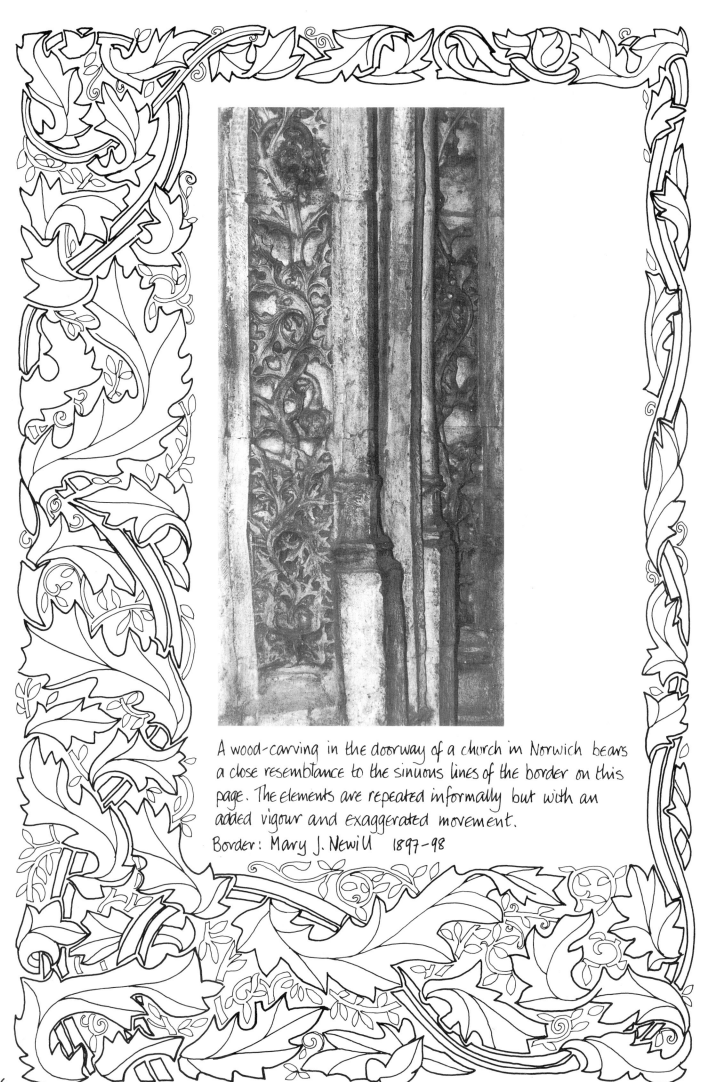

A wood-carving in the doorway of a church in Norwich bears
a close resemblance to the sinuous lines of the border on this
page. The elements are repeated informally but with an
added vigour and exaggerated movement.

Border: Mary J. Newill   1897–98

Top: an 18th century-style garland. Often moulded in plaster or carved in wood.

Left and centre: border designs by Benedictus.

Right: from a Chinese Cizhou jar of 12th – 13th centuries.

18th century Japanese.

English Queen. c. 1380

above: Art Nouveau head-dress in the style of Alphonse Mucha.

Byzantine. 6th century

Egyptian musicians from an 18th. dynasty tomb at Thebes. 14th C. B.C.

Ficticious head-dress.
Vaguely eastern.
One of the three magi,
perhaps?

Gilt bronze helmet, a replica of
the Sutton Hoo helmet probably
worn by a warrior king.
British Museum.
Anglo-Saxon.

Bronze head, probably King
Sargon I of Akkad from
Nineveh, c. 2350 B.C.
Now in Iraq Museum.
Baghdad.

Minoan hairstyle c. 1450 B.C.

A bas-relief
showing the head of a Hitite
goddess wearing a high polos
surmounted by a veil.
8th century B.C.

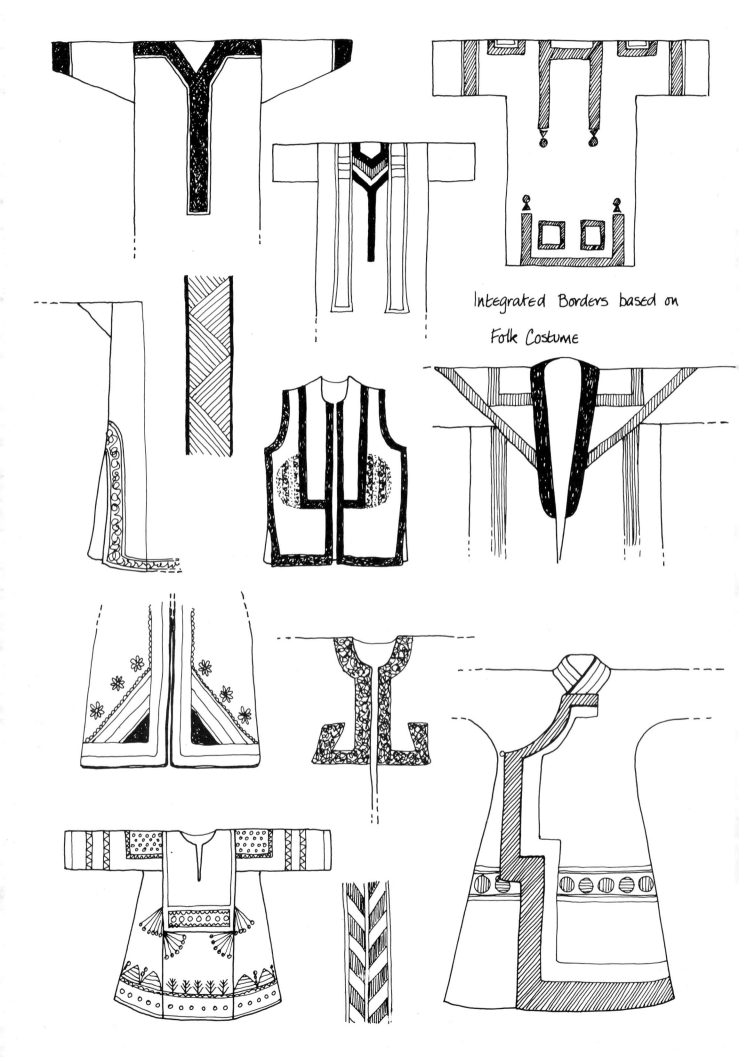

Integrated Borders based on

Folk Costume